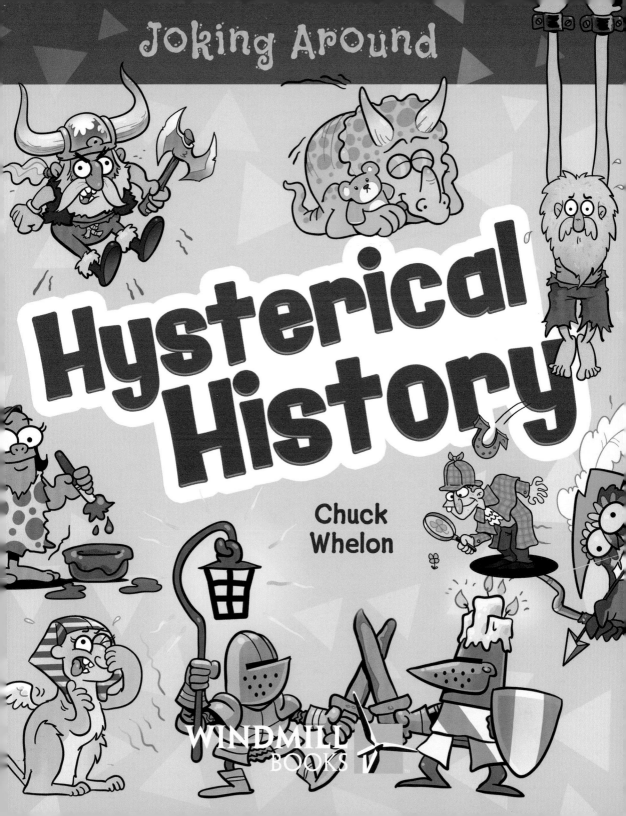

Published in 2019 by Windmill Books,
an Imprint of Rosen Publishing
29 East 21st Street, New York, NY 10010

Editors: Samantha Hilton and Joe Harris, with Julia Adams
Book Design: Stefan Holiland, with Emma Randall

Photo Credits:

Key: b-bottom, t-top, c-center, l-left, r-right
Chuck Wheldon: cover, 1, 3br, 4bl, 5b, 6b, 7b, 8tl, 9tl, 10bl, 11br, 12cr, 12bl, 13tl, 14bl, 15br, 16br, 17bl, 18b, 19b, 20bl, 21bl, 22br; Shutterstock/Memo Angeles: 3cr, 4tl, 5tc, 6tr, 7tr, 8bc, 9bl, 10cr, 11tc, 13bc, 14cr, 15tr, 16tl, 17tr, 18tl, 19tr, 20tr, 21t, 22tl, 23tc, 23bl, 24tc, 24bl, 25tl, 25br, 26tl, 26bl, 27tl, 27br, 28tr, 28bc, 29tc, 29bc.

Cataloging-in-Publication Data

Names: Whelon, Chuck.
Title: Hysterical history / Chuck Whelon.
Description: New York : Windmill Books, 2019. | Series: Joking around
Identifiers: LCCN ISBN 9781508195641 (pbk.) | ISBN 9781508195634 (library bound) |
ISBN 9781508195658 (6 pack)
Subjects: LCSH: History--Juvenile humor.
Classification: LCC PN6231.H47 W48 2019 | DDC 808.88'2--dc23

Manufactured in the United States of America

CPSIA Compliance Information: Batch #BS18WM: For Further Information contact Rosen Publishing, New York, New York at 1-800-237-9932

What was the first thing said by the inventor of the stink bomb?

"You reek, ugh!"

Say this three times, quickly.

Two terrible T. rex wreck trains together!

Who succeeded the first President of the United States?

The second one!

What do you call a sleeping Triceratops?

A dino-shore!

4

What invention lets you see through walls?

The window!

How do you find Tutankhamun's tomb?

Peer-amid the other tombs!

Why does the Statue of Liberty stand outside New York?

It can't sit down!

Need an ark to save two of every animal?

I Noah guy...

Which cat discovered America?

Christofur Columpaws!

What do you call a Roman emperor with a cold?

Julius Sneezer!

Why did Renoir become an Impressionist?

He did it for the Monet!

Say this three times, quickly.

Tutankhamun tucked twenty treasures in his tomb!

Why did everyone in nineteenth-century England carry an umbrella?

Because Queen Victoria's reign lasted for 64 years!

What movie did the ancient Greeks like best?

Troy Story!

Why can't you hear a pterodactyl going to the bathroom?

Because the "p" is silent!

Which famous gunfighter had indigestion?

Wyatt Burp!

What happened to the royal chicken that couldn't lay eggs?

The king had her eggs-ecuted!

Did you hear about the card game on Noah's Ark?

It was ruined by a cheetah!

Which owl robbed the rich to give to the poor?

Robin Hoot!

What do history teachers talk about on dates?

The good old days!

Who made King Arthur's round table?

Sir Cumference!

What is the fruitiest subject at school?

History, because it's full of dates!

How was the Roman empire divided?

With a pair of Caesars!

Which figure in history ate the most?

Attila the Hungry!

Why were the ancient Egyptians so unhappy with their ruler?

Because he was being un-Pharaoh!

Say this three times, quickly.

Cunning Cleopatra's clever scheming charmed Caesar!

What happened when electricity was first discovered?

People got a nasty shock!

Knock, knock.

Who's there?

Robin.

Robin who?

Robin the rich to give to the poor!

Why was the ancient Egyptian mummy so tense?

He was always wound up!

Which emperor should have stayed away from gunpowder?

Napoleon Blownapart!

What do you call a fortunate detective?

Sheerluck Holmes!

How did pharaohs get the best pyramids?

They asked for a tomb with a view!

What was Robin Hood's mother called?

Mother Hood!

Which monarch had the worst skin?

Mary, Queen of Spots!

What is a forum?

Two-um plus two-um!

What do you call a frog who wants to be a cowboy?

Hop-along Cassidy!

Why did the student miss the history exam?

He had the wrong date!

Which famous explorer was good at sports?

Marco Polo!

Where did King Arthur's men get their training?

Knight school!

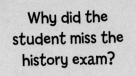

Did you hear about the unembalmed ancient Egyptian discovery?

It sphinx!

How did Robin Hood steal from the rich?

He pulled some purse strings!

What happened when the wheel was invented?

It started a revolution!

Where was the Declaration of Independence signed?

At the bottom!

Which fruit launched a thousand ships?

Melon of Troy!

What did Henry VIII do whenever he burped?

He issued a Royal Pardon!

Try saying this three times, quickly.

Upon the placid plains, the Pawnee ponies pranced!

What do you call a friendly pharaoh?

A chummy mummy!

What did the executioner shout to the line of prisoners?

"Necks, please!"

Knock, knock.
Who's there?
Jester.
Jester who?
Jester wondering if you were at home!

What do you get if you cross a Roman emperor with a boa constrictor?

Julius Squeezer!

What was Queen Victoria's most treasured item of clothing?

Her reign-coat!

What creature hunted in prehistoric oceans?

Jurassic shark!

Did you hear about the Shakespearean actor who fell through the floor?

It was a just a stage he was going through!

What do you call a Roman emperor who has adventures?

An action Nero!

Why did cave people paint pictures of hippopotamuses?

They couldn't spell it!

HIPPYPITTAMICE

HYPOPOTTYMOUTH

HAPPYPOTATOMAS

Why were the Dark Ages so confusing?

It was common to hear, "Good morning, good knight"!

Why did the archer change his career?

He found his work too arrowing!

Knock, knock.

Who's there?

Julius.

Julius who?

Julius, seize her! She took my wallet!

Riddle me this!

I'm a sea where Egyptian mummies like to swim. What am I?

The Dead Sea.

Did you hear about the queen whose eldest son disobeyed her?

She was having a bad heir day!

What was the prisoner doing in the medieval dungeon?

Just hanging!

Who said, "Cluck, cluck!" and conquered half the world?

Attila the Hen!

How did Noah navigate in the dark?

With floodlights!

What did Anne Boleyn's lady-in-waiting say on her wedding day?

"That man's not worth losing your head over!"

What sweet treat did cavemen like the best?

Spearmints!

How did people tie their shoelaces in the Middle Ages?

With a longbow!

Why did the cowboy choose his horse in broad daylight?

He didn't want a night-mare!

Why wouldn't the ancient Egyptian accept that his boat was sinking?

He was in de-Nile!

Why did the hangman's wife ask for a divorce?

Her husband was a pain in the neck!

What kind of dinosaur can you ride in a rodeo?

A Bronco-saurus!

Riddle me this. People could catch me, but they couldn't throw me. What am I?

The plague.

Why is it no fun being an archaeologist?

Your career is always in ruins!

What did the dragon say when it saw Sir Lancelot?

"Ugh, more canned food!"

Which Roman emperor was the coolest?

Julius Freezer!

Which knight was King Arthur's best bodyguard?

Sir Curity!

What kind of socks did pirates wear?

Arrr-gyle!

Nero: What time is it?

Servant: X past VII!

How did Christopher Columbus get to college?

On a scholar-ship!

Which famous knight never won a battle?

Sir Endor!

Which animal discovered the Internet?

The beaver—it was the first to log on!

Who do archaeologists invite to their parties?

Anyone they can dig up!

9.99

In which battle was Genghis Khan killed?

His last one!

Why did everyone laugh at the cowboy?

He was always horsing around!

What comes once in a minute, twice in a moment, but never in a thousand years?

The letter "m."

Say this three times, quickly.

Caesar saw his sister sitting on a seesaw!

Did you hear about the mummy that lost its temper?

It flipped its lid!

Where did Montezuma go to college?

Az Tech!

What were Julius Sneezer's dying words?

"Achoo, Brute!"

Why did Eve want to move to New York?

She wanted to see the Big Apple!

Why did the dragon spit out the court jester?

Because he tasted funny!

What kind of king wears a horned crown?

A Vi-king!

Which Russian leader was a big fan of fruit?

Peter the Grape!

Which ancient people moved around the most?

The Roam-ans!

Why were the ancient Egyptians good at spying?

They kept things under wraps!

Did you hear about the T. rex that ate a firework?

It was dinomite!

Say this three times, quickly.

Sly pirates spy pilots buying pies!

Why was King Arthur's table round?
So he couldn't be cornered!

Who was Wyatt Burp's best friend?
Wild Bill Hiccup!

Was Rome built in a day?
No, it was built in Italy!

Why did cavemen love to eat sloths?
They knew that fast food was bad for you!

What do you call a dinosaur with no eyes?

Doyouthinkhesaurus!

What does an executioner read in the morning?

The noose-paper!

When in history did people have the nicest, smoothest clothes?

During the Iron Age!

What did Sir Lancelot's mother say to him at bedtime?

"Knight, knight!"

Which king invented fractions?

Henry the $\frac{1}{8}$!

How did cavemen make fire with two sticks?

They made sure one was a match!

What letters are like a Roman emperor?

The "Cs" are!

Say this three times, quickly!

Robin Hood robbed the rich of their riches until King Rich's return!

When did the Vikings make their raids?

During a plunder storm!

What was T. rex's lucky number?

Eight!

What loses its head in the morning but gets it back at night?

A pillow!

Say this three times, quickly.

On various voyages, vile Vikings revolted violently!

Say this three times, quickly.

Sir Lancelot, please dance a lot! Thanks a lot.

What do kings and queens drink at breakfast?

Royal-tea!

Which knight was King Arthur's best lookout?

Sir Veillance!

What was written on the knight's tomb?

"Rust in Peace"!

Say this three times, quickly.

The Queen's birthday is the third Thursday of this month!

Glossary

archaeologist A scientist who researches the history of wildlife and humans by studying artifacts and fossils.

argyle A diamond-shaped pattern used in clothing, such as socks and sweaters.

Aztecs A people who settled in a part of Mexico in the 13th century.

Boleyn, Anne The Queen of England from 1533 until she was beheaded in 1536. She was the second wife of Henry VIII, and mother of Elizabeth, later to be crowned Elizabeth I.

bronco An untrained horse, often used in rodeos.

Camelot The legendary castle of King Arthur.

embalm To preserve a dead body with spices or chemicals.

forum In ancient Rome, a public space in a city where people met to exchange ideas, and where markets took place.

horse around To fool around.

jester In the Middle Ages, someone who was employed to entertain the royal court.

Khan, Genghis A ruler, warrior, and conqueror who founded Mongolia in the early 13th century.

Monet, Claude French Impressionist painter who lived 1840-1926.

Montezuma II Aztec emperor who lived 1466-1520.

Norse In the Middle Ages, someone or something from Norway or Scandinavia.

Peter the Great Peter I, emperor of Russia who reigned from 1682-1725.

polo A team sport played on horseback.

pterodactyl A prehistoric flying reptile.

Renoir, Pierre-Auguste French Impressionist painter who lived 1841-1919.

revolution A rebellion or complete change; one complete turn of a wheel.

Sir Lancelot A knight who features in the legends of King Arthur.

Triceratops A large, plant-eating dinosaur that lived during the Cretaceous period.

Tutankhamun A king of ancient Egypt who ruled 1333-23 BCE and whose intact tomb was discovered in 1922.

Further Information

Books:

Deary, Terry. *Crackin' Castles* (Horrible Histories). London, UK: Scholastic, 2016.

Leedy, Loreen. *My Teacher Is a Dinosaur, and Other Prehistoric Poems, Jokes, Riddles, and Amazing Facts.* New York: Two Lions, 2014.

Milligan, Spike. *Silly Verse for Kids.* London, UK: Puffin, 2015.

Robinson, Sir Tony. *Sir Tony Robinson's Weird World of Wonders Joke Book: Hysterical, Historical Jokes and Facts.* London, UK: Macmillan Children's Books, 2017.

Vine, Tim. *The (Not Quite) Biggest Ever Time Vine Joke Book: Children's Edition.* London, UK: Red Fox, 2011.

For web resources related to the subject of this book, go to: www.windmillbooks.com/weblinks and select this book's title.

Index